Stories for Three-Year-Olds

Other Story Collections in this Series:

Stories for Three-Year-Olds

by

Amanda Benjamin,
Tony Bradman,
Fiona Cummings,
Andrew Donkin,
David Morton,
Paul Ress,
Jane Tait
and Polly Whittacker

Illustrated by Sami Sweeten

First published in Great Britain by
CollinsChildren'sBooks 1996

1 3 5 7 9 8 6 4 2

CollinsChildren'sBooks is a division of
HarperCollins*Publishers* Ltd
77–85 Fulham Palace Road
Hammersmith, London W6 8JB

Printed and bound in Great Britain by
Caledonian International Book Manufacturing Limited, Glasgow

ISBN 0 00 675238-1

CONTENTS

(The times in brackets show approximately how long it takes
to read each story aloud.)

JAKE AND THE BATH TIME PIRATES
by Andrew Donkin

Jake's bath had pirates.

Every bath time the pirates' big ship appeared, sailing through the bubbles that floated on the surface of the water.

All of Jake's other bath toys were scared of the pirate ship. It was longer than his submarine, taller than his green plastic frog and faster than his clockwork penguin. But Jake wasn't scared of it – he liked it best of all.

This bath time, Jake's dad couldn't find the shampoo. While he was rummaging in the cupboard, Jake wound up the clockwork penguin. It paddled across the water with its big hollow belly in the air until… splash! …it bumped into the plastic frog.

"Watch it!" croaked the frog, bobbing up and down.

Just then the pirate ship

appeared.

"Ahoy there, Admiral Jake," yelled the captain.

Jake quickly saluted, sending a wave of foam over the deck.

"What's the plan, Captain?" he asked.

"Treasure," replied the captain.

"I haven't got any treasure for you today," said Jake.

"I don't want any *more* treasure," said the captain. "I want a good hiding place for all *this* treasure."

Jake leaned forward and looked inside the ship. In the hold he saw the pirate captain's treasure – three coins, two buttons, a piece of silver paper, a pen top and four Smarties.

"Got any ideas?" asked the captain.

Jake thought very hard.

"What about hiding it in a secret underwater cave?" he said.

He felt all around the sides of the bath, but he couldn't find any secret underwater caves.

Then Jake said, "What about hiding it in a shipwreck at the bottom of the ocean?"

He felt all along the bottom of the bath, but he couldn't find any shipwrecks either.

Just then Jake's dad found the shampoo and brought it over to the bath. When he saw the pirate ship he saluted and asked, "What's the

mission today?"

"Treasure," said the pirate captain.

"I haven't any treasure today," said Dad. "You've had my coins, and the buttons off my shirt. If you want more treasure you'll have to fight for it!"

The pirate captain became very excited. "Water fight! Water fight!" he shouted running up and down the deck.

The other bath toys began paddling towards the taps, to get out of the way. Even Jake moved back a bit.

"If he wants a water fight, he shall have one," said the plastic

pirate captain, forgetting all about
the treasure.

Running to the side of the deck,
he aimed one of the ship's water
cannons. Whoosh! Water shot out
and hit Dad on the shoulder. The
next shot got him on the ear.

"Right. That's it," said Dad.

He grabbed an empty squeezy
bottle and dipped it in the bath.
Then he aimed it carefully.

Splooosh! The water sloshed over
the pirate ship.

Dad fired again. Splot! This time
he hit the pirate captain and
knocked off his hat.

"Shiver me timbers!" shouted the
captain as it flew overboard.

Jake giggled as water flew in every direction. Left, right, up, down, sideways. Everywhere!

Finally the captain decided he'd try one last trick. He turned the ship sharply around, making a huge wave in the water. The wave headed towards the end of the bath.

"Ha ha!" yelled Dad, thinking he'd won.

Then the wave hit the end of the bath and started to come back – only now it was much bigger.

"That's what waves do," shouted the captain to Jake. "They come back. Only bigger!"

The wave hit the side of the bath and whooshed all over Jake's dad.

It went in his eyes so he couldn't see.

It went down his ears so he couldn't hear.

It went up his nose so he couldn't smell anything (except, he said afterwards, soap).

"That's how to win a water fight, that is," cheered the captain proudly, hoisting his pirate flag.

Jake's dad was soaked.

"Help! I need to dry off!" he spluttered. "And it's time you were out of that bath," he added. With eyes tightly shut, he felt round the bathroom for a towel.

"Quick," said the pirate captain while Dad was busy. "We've still got to hide my treasure."

Jake looked around. Where could they hide it? His other bath toys had been sunk by the big wave – all except the clockwork penguin with his big belly.

"Got it!" said Jake. He picked up the penguin and flipped open his tummy. Inside was a big empty space – just right for hiding treasure!

"Perfect," said the captain as Jake quickly piled the treasure inside. "Look after it for me," he added, turning his ship around and sailing away.

Just in time!

Dad's head appeared from under

the towel. He reached over and pulled out the bath plug. Then he hoisted Jake out of the bath, wrapped him in the towel and gave him a big, wet hug.

As the water gurgled away the penguin smiled to himself.

"When everyone has gone," he thought, "I'll make a run for it with the treasure."

But he never did. He was too full to move.

EMMY'S BIRTHDAY FISH
by Amanda Benjamin

It was Emmy's birthday. She sat on
the sunny kitchen steps listening to
her mum making breakfast. It was
her favourite – boiled egg and toast
soldiers.

Just then the cat from next door jumped down from the garden wall and padded over the grass. He stopped at the edge of the fish pond and stared into the water.

Emmy knew what that fat old cat was thinking. He was thinking how tasty one of those fish would be for his breakfast. But Emmy knew he would never catch one of them. They were far too quick and clever for such a lazy old cat. Her big brother Tod had told her that.

Emmy loved watching the fish. She wasn't allowed to go to the pond by herself, but every day she asked Tod or her mum or her dad to take her there to see the fish.

When Emmy went indoors for breakfast, Tod was already at the table. Her dad caught her in his arms and swung her in the air.

"Happy birthday!" everyone called.

Then Emmy's eyes opened wide. There, next to her chair, was a shiny red tricycle. But there was something else, too. On the table was a big glass bowl full of water. And in the bowl was a fish.

"It's from me!" shouted Tod. "It's your very own goldfish."

Emmy pressed her nose against the glass of the bowl. Her fish was beautiful – gold, with a soft wavy tail.

"Hello fish," said Emmy.

The fish blew two big bubbles.

"He can't talk," laughed Tod.

But Emmy was sure the fish had said something – it was just too quiet for anyone to hear.

"What's your name?" she whispered.

The fish blew more bubbles. His mouth made an 'oh' shape, as if he were saying, "Allo, allo."

"That's funny," Emmy laughed.

But the fish did not smile. He looked sad. His small pink mouth opened and closed silently.

Emmy put her fingers on the glass.

"I can't hear you," she said.

All that day, Emmy played with her new tricyle. But she kept going back to the goldfish bowl to listen very hard, trying to hear what the fish was saying.

At teatime, Emmy had a fat pink cake with three stripy candles. Emmy's mum lit them and, as Emmy leaned forward to blow them out, Tod called, "Make a wish. Quick!"

Emmy took a deep breath, closed her eyes tightly and blew. She wished she could hear what her fish was saying.

That night, after her story, Emmy snuggled up in her bed and thought about her fish.

She wondered where he came from and who his friends were.

"I wonder what it's like to be a fish," she murmured, and as she was wondering, she fell asleep.

Emmy dreamed she was swimming in a big glass bowl. She saw something big and golden swimming towards her. She knew it was her fish, but now they were almost the same size.

"Hello Emmy," said the fish. His bubble whispers were soft, but she could hear them clearly.

"I knew you could speak," cried Emmy. As she spoke, she saw bubbles coming from her own mouth.

"Come and swim with me," said the fish. And as they swam he told her fishy stories, about playing hide and seek with his brothers and sisters, of chasing in and out of the dark weeds and blowing bubbles at the world above.

When Emmy woke up next morning she remembered her dream and called her mum.

"Mum, I want to put my fish into the pond," she said.

"Your birthday fish!" exclaimed her mum. "But you might never see him again."

"He's got no one to talk to or play with," insisted Emmy. "Please!"

Emmy ran downstairs to the

kitchen. There was the fish. She put her fingers on the glass and the fish swam to them.

"Allo, allo," he bubbled.

"Hello," replied Emmy. "We're going to the pond."

Very gently, Emmy's mum put the fish bowl in the basket of Emmy's new tricycle and they wheeled it slowly down the garden path to the fish pond. Then they carefully tipped the fish into the water. With a splash, he disappeared.

"Well, there he goes," said Emmy's mum. "Come on, darling."

But Emmy waited. She knew the fish was down in the lovely dark weeds, playing hide and seek with his new friends.

Just then there was a ripple and a splash in the pond, and quick as a flash a fish's nose popped out of the water.

It was her fish, Emmy knew it! She listened very hard and thought she almost heard a tiny whispered, "Thank you!" Then he splashed his tail and was gone.

Emmy still went to the fish pond every day, with her mum or dad or Tod. And whenever she went, one fish would always swim to the top of the water and blow bubbles as if to say, "Allo, allo!"

JASPER THE DRAGON
by David Morton

Jasper the little dragon lived at the top of a very high mountain, with his mother and father and baby sister.

He was just like any other dragon you might know. He was green and scaly. He could fly in the air, backwards and forwards – he could even turn somersaults and fly upside down. And he could roar that terrible dragon roar:

"ROAAAAAAR!
   ROAAAAAAAR!
      ROAAAAAAAAAR!"

But there was one dragon thing that Jasper couldn't do – he couldn't breathe fire.

Now, all dragons can breathe fire – even the teeniest, tiniest dragon. In fact, Jasper's baby sister was really good at it. But no matter how hard Jasper tried, he couldn't do it. Not enough to light a candle. Not even a puff of smoke.

"Why can't I breathe fire?" Jasper asked his mum. "I keep on huffing and puffing, but nothing ever happens."

"Don't worry about it," comforted his mother. "You're probably trying too hard. Just forget about it and one day you'll find you can do it. All dragons can breathe fire, you know."

But Jasper couldn't forget about it and he kept on trying. He huffed in his garden and he puffed in the playground. He huffed in his bedroom and he puffed in the kitchen. He even practised breathing fire when he was in the bathroom! But nothing ever happened – except that Jasper got very puffed out.

One day, Jasper was so fed up with trying to breathe fire that he decided to run away. He flapped his wings and flew down the mountain, right to the bottom, where he landed in a large field. It was the perfect place to practise breathing fire, but Jasper was too unhappy to even try.

"It's no good, I'll never be a proper dragon," Jasper cried. "Everyone will laugh at me."

And feeling very sorry for himself, he began to sob.

Just then, a little girl called Rebecca came by. Now, Rebecca knew all about dragons. She knew that they were green and scaly. She knew that they could fly in the air, backwards and forwards – even turn somersaults and fly upside down. She knew that they could roar a terrible dragon roar:

"ROAAAAAAR!
ROAAAAAAAR!
ROAAAAAAAAAR!"

And Rebecca knew that absolutely *all* dragons breathed fire

and that she should be very scared
of them. However, when she
noticed Jasper crying in the middle
of the field, she thought that he
wasn't much like any of the
dragons she had heard about and
quite forgot to be scared.

"What's the matter?" she asked.

Jasper was sobbing so hard and
so loud that he didn't hear Rebecca
come up beside him and her
question made him jump.

"Go away," he sniffed, rather
rudely. "You're laughing at me
because I can't breathe fire."

"All dragons can breathe fire,"
replied Rebecca.

"Well I can't," wailed Jasper, "so

just go away."

"How rude!" exclaimed Rebecca. "I was going to offer to help you, but I don't think you deserve it."

Jasper looked up at her through his tears. "I'm sorry," he said. "It's just that I've been practising and practising breathing fire, but nothing ever happens."

"Perhaps you're trying too hard," suggested Rebecca.

"That's what my mum said," nodded Jasper, "but I just can't forget about it."

So Rebecca sat down next to the little dragon and together they tried to come up with some new ideas for Jasper to try. They had been thinking for nearly five whole minutes when Rebecca jumped up.

"I know," she said. "My dad says he thinks better when he's walking around. If I go for a walk it might help me think of a way to help you."

So, Rebecca started walking round the field. She was so busy thinking that she didn't see the big grey wolf creep out of the woods at the foot of the mountain, and she didn't see him lick his lips.

The wolf didn't see Jasper, but Jasper saw the wolf and it made him forget all about crying. Jasper had heard enough fairy tales to know that wolves ate little girls like

Rebecca for breakfast. He had to help her, but what could he do?

"Perhaps if I roar my terrible dragon roar, I might scare him and he'll run away," thought Jasper. So he stood up, took a very deep breath, and let out the biggest and most terrible dragon roar he could:

"ROAAAAAAR!
ROAAAAAAAR!
ROAAAAAAAAAAR!"

As he did so, an enormous sheet of fire came blasting out of Jasper's mouth. It flared through the grass until it reached the wolf, where it burnt the tip of his tail. *Sssszzzt!*

Howling and yowling, the wolf leapt high in the air. Then he ran off back to the woods as fast as he could and never dared poke his nose out of there again.

Jasper was the happiest dragon in the world. He and Rebecca became best friends and Jasper often took her flying on his back. Turning somersaults and flying upside down, roaring his terrible dragon roar and breathing fire – as all dragons do.

THE WIDE-AWAKE BOAT
by Polly Whittacker

Bridget never wanted to go to bed.

"Not sleepy," she told her mum,
and did a little dance to prove it.

"Come on, Bridget the Fidget,"
said Mum. "You'll be sleepy when
you've had your bath."

So Bridget went with Mum and had her bath. She pretended she was a mermaid floating in a sea of tropical bubbles until Mum pulled the plug out.

Then Mum wrapped her up in a big fluffy towel and carried her off to the bedroom.

"Not sleepy," said Bridget, kicking her feet and sending a puff of talcum powder into the air.

"Come on, Bridget the Fidget," said Mum. "You'll be sleepy when you've got your pyjamas on. Do you know where they are?"

So Bridget helped Mum to find her pyjamas. They were pink pyjamas, with pictures of sheep on.

Bridget pretended to be Little Bo Peep while they looked for them in the chest of drawers.

When Bridget had her pyjamas on, she climbed into her bed.

"Not sleepy," she insisted, doing roly-polys down the bed until the quilt fell off on to the floor.

"Come on, Bridget the Fidget," said Mum, unrolling Bridget and picking up the quilt. "You'll be sleepy when you've had your story."

Mum tucked Bridget tightly into her bed and read her a story about animals. Bridget pretended to be a caterpillar while she listened, but she still didn't feel sleepy.

After the story, Mum kissed Bridget goodnight.

"Not sleepy," she muttered, and fidgeted again.

"I know," said Mum, switching off the light, "I'll open the curtains so you can count the stars. Perhaps, if you look hard enough, you'll see the man in the moon."

So Bridget lay in bed, fidgeting. She looked out of the window where the black velvet sky was prickling with stars and felt more wide-awake than ever.

The moon was very bright as it shone into Bridget's bedroom. Bridget pretended that the moonlight was a river running out of the sky. She pretended that she could see a boat on the river, sailing out of the moon towards her.

All of a sudden, Bridget sat up and rubbed her eyes. There really *was* a boat, and it had just sailed through her bedroom window!

Sitting in the boat was a little silver man in a shiny suit. Bridget knew at once that he was a star.

"Come on, Bridget the Fidget," he said. "Come for a ride in the Wide-Awake Boat. You'll never go to sleep tonight."

Bridget looked in the boat and saw a soft cushion with her name on it, spelled out in shiny blue jewels.

"Oh yes," she laughed, and jumped into the boat. "What's your name?"

"Sparkle," replied the star, and turned the boat around.

Up into the air they swooped, bobbing up the river of moonbeams into the night sky. High above Bridget's head the stars twinkled merrily. Far below, beneath the boat, the lights from the houses and lamp posts grew smaller and smaller.

"Where are we going?" Bridget asked Sparkle.

"Following the river, up to the moon," he replied, and laughed a twinkling laugh that made the

Wide-Awake Boat jiggle up and down.

Bridget laughed too. "It tickles," she giggled, and fidgeted on her cushion.

The boat sailed on, higher and higher up the moonbeam river. Suddenly Bridget pointed.

"Look! The stars are moving!" she gasped.

"Well, we're awake all night long," said Sparkle. "We get fidgety, just like you."

As Bridget watched, the stars began to turn into things she knew. There was a mermaid sitting on a rock with dolphins darting around her tail. She waved to Bridget as the boat went by.

A little further on, Bridget saw Little Bo Peep chasing sheep round and round a pyjama tree, watched by a fat and lazy caterpillar lying in its branches.

"Let's go a bit faster," said Sparkle, and he blew gently into the silver sails. Up and up they went, and Bridget's long hair streamed out behind her like a tail.

"Now we look like a shooting star," cried the little man, laughing his twinkling laugh. Bridget the Fidget giggled and giggled.

Suddenly, up ahead, a bright white circle appeared.

"The moon! The moon!" Sparkle

called to Bridget.

"We're nearly there!" yelled Bridget. "Look! I can see the Man in the Moon!"

She was so excited she leapt to her feet.

"Look out, Bridget the Fidget!" shouted Sparkle.

But it was too late. The boat wiggled and jiggled, and bucked and bobbed, and tossed Bridget right out.

Down, down the river of moonbeams she slid. Past Little Bo Peep and the fat caterpillar, past the mermaid and her dolphins. Bridget shut her eyes tight. Down, down she went, faster and faster, until finally she landed with a bump!

"Come on, sleepyhead," said a voice. "Time to get up."

Bridget opened her eyes and, to her surprise, she found she was back in her own room. The sun was shining and her mum was smiling at the end of her bed.

After that, Bridget looked out for Sparkle and the Wide-Awake Boat every night. But she never saw them again – she was too busy sleeping.

THE RUDE RABBIT
by Jane Tait

It was playgroup day and Mary
didn't want to go. She squeezed her
mummy's hand tightly as they
walked to the door. When Mrs
Brooks, the teacher, opened the door,
Mary grabbed her mummy's leg.

"Come on, Mary," said Mrs Brooks. "Come and play in the sandpit."

Mary started to cry. When Mrs Brooks took her hand, Mary screamed and tried to run out of the door. So Mrs Brooks picked her up and put her by the toybox.

"Now Mary," she said, "I'll go and put your coat away. Why don't you choose a nice fluffy toy to play with."

Mary took a deep breath and was about to scream again when a voice said, "Oh, do be quiet! You're giving me a headache."

Mary was so surprised she forgot to scream. There in front of her was a small blue rabbit with his paws over his ears. He looked up at Mary and stuck out his tongue.

Mary giggled. "You're rude, she said.

"That's better," grinned the rabbit. "I hate screaming."

Just then, Mrs Brooks came back.

"Feeling better, Mary?" she said kindly.

The blue rabbit made a horrid face and a rude noise. Mary giggled again.

"Good girl, Mary," smiled Mrs Brooks. "You enjoy yourself." And off she went.

"My mummy says it's naughty to be rude," said Mary to the rabbit.

"Well your mummy's not here," he answered.

Mary's lip began to wobble, but before she could start crying the rude rabbit jumped into her arms.

"Take me to the sandpit!" he ordered. "I want to knock over some sandcastles."

So Mary carried him over to the sandpit.

A little boy was already playing in the sand. He glared at Mary.

"My name is William," he said, "and you're a cry baby."

"I'm not!" said Mary.

"Are!" said William.

While they were arguing the rude rabbit kicked over William's

sandcastle.

"Ha ha!" he chuckled. "Tell him he's got a big bottom, too!"

Mary decided it was time to do something else. She took the rude rabbit to the painting table. Mary painted a picture of the rabbit with his tongue sticking out.

"That's good," said the rabbit. "Now paint a picture of me doing something really naughty."

Just then William came over and looked at the painting.

"That's yukky," he said crossly. "I'm much better at painting." And he painted a picture of a big red house.

The rude rabbit winked at Mary

and knocked blue paint all over William's picture when he wasn't looking.

Although Mary didn't really like William, she was a bit shocked at the rabbit's naughtiness. She didn't quite know what to do, so she took the rabbit back to the toy box before William could blame her for spoiling his picture.

"It's tidy-up time now, children!" called Mrs Brooks. "Everybody clear up!"

William started to put all the building bricks neatly into a box. The rude rabbit winked at Mary again and, behind William's back, he began to take them all out again.

"William!" said Mrs Brooks. "Tidy the bricks away in the box, please. It's time to stop playing."

Poor William had to start all over again. Mary was beginning to feel sorry for him.

Then it was time for milk and biscuits.

"Here, Mary," said Mrs Brooks giving her a drink. "Sit next to William."

"Oh, goody!" said the rude rabbit. He took a straw and drank up every last drop of William's milk. Then he patted his tummy and gave a huge burp.

"He really *is* rude," thought Mary, "and he's very naughty."

William started to cry. Mary
pushed her milk over to him.

"Here you are," she said kindly.
"You can share my milk."

William stared at her in surprise,
then took a big drink of milk.

"Thank you," he said in a small
voice and sniffed.

The rude rabbit snorted. "Now
who's a cry baby!" he said.

But Mary ignored him – she was
too busy talking to William.

When Mary's mother arrived to
pick her up, she was amazed to see
Mary so happy.

"Well!" she said. "You look as if
you've had a good time!"

The next playgroup day, Mary

rushed in and ran straight to the toybox. She took out all the fluffy toys, but the rude rabbit was nowhere to be found.

"Where's the blue rabbit, Mrs Brooks?" she asked.

"I don't think there is a *blue* rabbit," replied her teacher. "Only brown ones."

So Mary went off to play in the sand pit. After all, William was a much better friend than the rude rabbit!

BLAKE AND HAYLEY BAILEY GO SHOPPING
by Paul Ress

Blake and Hayley Bailey loved to go shopping with their mum. Every Monday afternoon they would march to the car and drive to the red brick supermarket building.

The first thing they did was to go to the bottle banks to throw away their old bottles. They loved the clinking and crashing sounds as the bottles fell into the big plastic bins. Blake and Hayley wished that they were tall enough to reach the holes, but sometimes Mum would lift them up so that they could have a turn at dropping in the bottles.

Then it was time to go into the shop. Blake and Hayley thought it was the most wonderful place. There were thousands of things to see and touch, and it always smelled of bananas and doughnuts. Blake loved bananas. Hayley loved doughnuts.

Hayley, who was three years old, always sat in the trolley. She pretended to be the Captain of a big plane. Blake pushed the trolley, making noises like a big propeller engine.

That day, they'd just walked through the entrance when Mum met Mrs Green. Blake and Hayley knew exactly what this meant – the grown-ups would talk and talk about all sorts of boring things instead of doing shopping.

Sure enough, the grown-ups talked. They talked and talked. And talked and talked and talked.

Captain Hayley, sitting in the trolley, began kicking her feet. "Go shopping," she said.

Blake looked up at her. "Shall we start?" he said. "Mum can catch up."

Hayley nodded excitedly. "Engine fly fast," she ordered.

So Blake quietly pulled at the trolley and off they flew down the smooth wide aisle.

Hayley pointed Blake in the direction of the bananas, but on the way they passed an enormous stack of tins.

"Beans!" yelled Hayley as they sped past.

Blake stopped the trolley. "Mum never buys enough beans," he said and began handing tins up to

Hayley.

When there were lots of tins of beans in the trolley, Blake started his trolley-plane again and headed off round the next aisle to find the bananas. He didn't get far.

"Food for Victor!" shrieked Hayley, pointing to the cat food.

"Good idea," said Blake, and stopped the trolley again. They had their beans – it was only fair that their cat Victor should have plenty of food too.

However, when Blake started picking up the big tins of cat food his mother usually bought, Captain Hayley stopped him.

"Pink tins," she insisted, pointing

at the special little cans which Victor sometimes had as a treat.

"Okay," nodded Blake. "But we'll have to get twice as many."

A pile of pink tins joined the pile of bean tins in the trolley, then they were off again in search of bananas.

The trolley-plane rounded another corner and nearly crashed into the bakery.

"Doughnuts! Doughnuts!" whooped Hayley.

There were packets of jam doughnuts and iced doughnuts, ring doughnuts and chocolate doughnuts. Blake and Hayley didn't know which ones to choose, so they decided to get some of each.

Into the trolley they went, on top of the tins of cat food and beans.

Off they went again, until Hayley yelled, "Paper for Dad."

"Good idea," said Blake, stopping by the newspaper stand. "I know, I'll buy a whole lot of newspapers so Dad won't have to get them delivered every morning."

The newspapers went into the trolley, on top of the doughnuts and the cat food and the beans.

The trolley was now nearly full and Blake was finding it very hard to steer. He had to stop making engine noises and just push with all his strength.

At last they came to the bananas.

Nothing else could fit into the trolley, so Blake filled Hayley's arms with all the bananas she could hold.

"Do you think we've got everything, Captain?" asked Blake.

Hayley thought for a minute and then nodded.

"Home," she ordered.

Slowly, Blake pushed the loaded trolley back to where they had started from, where Mum was still talking busily to Mrs Green.

Just in time! Mum turned round and said, "Come on, Blake and Hayley, let's go and do the shopping.

"It's okay, Mum," said Blake.

"We've done it all," laughed Hayley.

Mum looked at the trolley packed full of baked beans, cat food, doughnuts, newspapers and bananas – and didn't know what to say!

A BAD WEEK FOR THE THREE BEARS
by Tony Bradman

It was Monday at the Bears' House,
And the week had just begun,
Father was cooking the breakfast
(The porridge was quite over-done).

Mother was laying the table,
Junior played on the floor,
When all of a sudden the family
  heard
A knocking upon the front door.

The postman had brought them a
  letter,
Some bills and a postcard or two.
There was one from the library lady,
Saying three books were long
  overdue.

The bills seemed to be in red writing,
Telling Father to pay straight away.
From then on he looked rather
  grumpy,
And didn't have that much to say.

The rest of the day wasn't too bad,
Except that it started to rain,
And Junior said that he didn't like
   school
And wouldn't go back there again.

He kicked and he screamed, and he
   shouted,
As they bundled him into the car,
They took him to school very
   quickly
(Thank goodness it wasn't too far!)

On Tuesday the bears were up early,
Said Father, "Let's start fresh and
  bright.
I'm sure that today will be
  smashing!
Just wait. You'll see that I'm right!"

Father was cooking the porridge.
Mother was sipping her tea.
The door opened wide and Junior
  arrived:
"Look out, everybody! It's me!"

Smashed crockery littered the lino.
Porridge slid down Father's cheeks.
Mother was shouting at Junior,
Who tried very hard to look meek.

The rest of the day wasn't too bad,
Except that the washing machine
Broke down and flooded the kitchen
(And turned all the clothes slightly
   green).

A bear who came out to repair it
Found a toy stuffed under the drum.
Mother called Junior for ages,
But for some reason he wouldn't
   come.

Breakfast on Wednesday was
   peaceful,
Everything seemed to go well.
Even Junior behaved himself,
Then Mother said, "What can I
   smell?"

Father rushed into the kitchen.
Smoke billowed out of the door.
He grabbed the porridge pot off the
  stove…
Then dropped it in pain, with a roar.

He hopped round the table holding
  his paw.
He called the pot several rude
  names.
Junior said that he'd heard them
  before
And used them at school in his
  games.

The rest of the day wasn't too bad,
Except that it started to rain,
And the car broke down on the way
  to school
And on the way home again.

Father looked under the bonnet.
He became an extremely wet bear.
Mother called out The Bears' Rescue
  Truck.
They charged quite a lot for repairs.

Father got up late on Thursday…
And then he went straight back to
  bed.
He couldn't stop sneezing and
  coughing,
And complained of an ache in the
  head.

Mother phoned up for the doctor,
Whe said Father had a bad cold,
Then told him he ought to be careful
Now he was getting quite old.

The rest of the day wasn't too bad,
Except for the noise Junior made.
He pretended that he was a soldier,
With a gun and several grenades.

Father was better on Friday
Breakfast was perfect as well,
Mother declared that the weather
    looked good,
As far as she could tell.

The postman arrived at 8.30
With bills and a letter or two;
The library lady was angry.
Those books were still overdue.

The rest of the day wasn't too bad,
Except at Junior's home time.
He brought a report from his teacher,
Which gave a long list of his crimes.

"Naughty," the teacher had written,
"Cheeky," and "Really quite bad!
Your cub is completely unbearable
I think that he's driving me mad!"

On Saturday breakfast was…
  different.
Junior was in disgrace.
Father walked up and down talking,
A very cross look on his face.

At last Mother put out the porridge,
Father got spoons from the drawer,
When all of a sudden the family
  heard
A knocking upon the front door.

Grimly, a constable stood there.
He said that there'd been a phone
  call.
Someone had broken a window.
Someone who wasn't that tall.

Father turned round and growled,
  "Junior…"
But the bear cub had quite
  disappeared.
Father went upstairs and got him.
He gripped him by one of his ears.

The constable gave him a caution.
"He's probably quite a good lad…
I blame the parents who let cubs run
  wild;
No wonder that some turn out bad."

Junior was sent to his bedroom.
He didn't get honey for tea.
His parents then tried to relax for a
  while,
They sat down to watch some TV.

They turned on their favourite
   programme,
But suddenly there was a smell.
"Is that smoke over there?" said
   Mother.
"Oh no, not the TV as well."

The TV set hissed… then exploded.
But Father soon put out the flames.
Junior mentioned he'd hit the set
   twice
That morning in one of his games.

Father, mouth open, was silent.
Junior apologised fast.
Mother just sank to her knees and
    said,
"How long is this week going to
    last?"

The rest of the day wasn't too bad.
Except that poor Father was ill.
His throat still felt quite peculiar,
So he took a very large pill.

Mother said she had a headache,
Then Father woke up in the night.
He'd had a bad dream about
    porridge,
Which gave him a terrible fright.

On Sunday the bears had a lie-in.
They just didn't want to get up.
At breakfast the trouble came early.
Junior broke Father's cup.

Then Father ruined the porridge.
It tasted like bowls of burnt cork.
"I can't eat this stuff," he said
    glumly.
"I know, let's go for a walk."

In minutes the bears were all ready.
They set out in search of some fun.
The forest was full of birds singing.
Above was a warm summer sun.

They strolled through the woods
and were happy.
Junior behaved as he should.
"Ah, this is the life," remarked
Father.
"Everything seems pretty good."

"The week hasn't really been *that*
bad.
And nothing can happen today.
I think I feel ready for breakfast
now…
Some porridge? What do you say?"

The rest of the day wasn't too bad.
They got home at 9.24.
But when they arrived they
     discovered
That someone had opened the door.

Let's leave the three bears and their
     story
As they push the front door with a
     creak.
Someone's upstairs, you know who
     that is.
And tomorrow begins a new week!

MESSY JESSIE
by Fiona Cummings

Jessie was always messy. Jessie
liked it that way. Her mummy did
not.

Her mummy always said, "Jessie,
you are so messy!" and sighed very
loudly.

But Jessie couldn't help it. When she saw a big puddle she had to jump right into the middle of it.

SPLASH! The water went all over her shoes and her socks and her dungarees. Jessie laughed and clapped and danced.

Her mummy sighed and said, "Jessie you are always so messy!"

When Jessie and her mummy saw a brass band playing in the park, Jessie had to join in – she couldn't help it. She pretended that her ice-cream cone was a trumpet and tried to play it.

TOOT, TOOT, TOOT! The ice-cream dribbled over her lips and her cheeks. It dripped down her blue dungarees in creamy smudges. Jessie giggled and licked her lips.

Her mummy sighed and said, "Jessie you are always so messy!" Then she got out a tissue and scrubbed Jessie's face.

At tea time Jessie had to tell her daddy about the band – she couldn't help it.

"This is what the drums sounded like," she said and banged her spoon on the table. BANG, BANG, BANG!

Jessie's spoon knocked over her drink. The orange juice spilt over her dungarees and the cup fell on to the floor. CRASH!

"Jessie, you are just too messy!"

said her mummy and daddy together.

One day it was Jessie's birthday and she was very excited. All her friends were coming to her party. There were going to be balloons and games and a cake with candles.

Before breakfast, Jessie opened her birthday presents. Her favourite was a train with a loud whistle. WHOO-WHOO! She also had a beautiful, floaty party dress. It was lovely – it looked just like a fairy's dress.

After breakfast, Jessie went out into the garden to play. She tried to water the plants with her daddy's watering-can. It was too heavy and instead of watering the plants, she spilt water all down her legs. SPLOSH!

Jessie giggled. Then she sat down on the wet ground and began to make mud pies. She couldn't help it!

"Oh Jessie, you are so messy!" sighed her mummy when she saw all the mud. "Right, upstairs for a bath!"

When she was clean, Jessie dressed in her party dress.

"Now Jessie," said her mummy, "You don't want to be messy in your lovely new dress. Do you think you can stay clean for once?"

Jessie nodded, but she wasn't

sure that she could. It was so easy
to get messy – she couldn't help it!

Then Jessie had an idea. She went
into the hall and carefully put on
her wellingtons and mackintosh.

Jessie went into the kitchen to
look at all the food for her party.
CLUNK! She tripped over the dog's
water bowl. The water sloshed over
the floor. Jessie's wellingtons got
very wet – but Jessie didn't.

Then Jessie saw the lovely red
jelly her mum had made for the
party tea. Jessie poked it to make it
wobble. It wibbled and wobbled.

Jessie giggled and poked it again.
This time it wibbled and wobbled
right down her front and on to the

floor.

When Jessie's mummy saw the mess she looked very cross. But when she saw Jessie dressed in her mackintosh and wellingtons she laughed – she couldn't help it! For on the outside, Jessie was very messy, but underneath her new party dress was lovely and clean.

"For once, you are not messy Jessie!" she smiled.

When Jessie's friends arrived she looked like a princess in her party dress. Everyone had lots of fun playing party games until it was time for tea.

Jessie liked the tea party best. There were big fat hot dogs with

squirty tomato sauce. There was
wobbly red jelly and sticky iced
buns. There were chocolate biscuits
and eggy sandwiches.

Everyone was having a
wonderful time, until Jessie looked
down at her party frock. It was
covered in tomato sauce, sticky
marks and chocolate smears.

Jessie thought she was going to
cry – she couldn't help it.

Then her mummy said, "Never
mind, Jessie. Everyone gets messy
at birthday teas."

When Jessie looked around at her
friends, she saw it was true.

"Why don't you go and put on
your dungarees," said Jessie's

mummy.

Jessie giggled. In her dungarees Jessie had the happiest, messiest birthday ever – she couldn't help it!